811.5 B798i

Bradbury, Ray, 1920-

I live by the invisible

DATE DUE

OCT 1 2 2006			

DEMCO 38-297

2 4 2003

I LIVE BY THE INVISIBLE

New & Selected Poems

Ray Bradbury

salmonpoetry

Published in 2002 by
Salmon Publishing Ltd,
Cliffs of Moher, Co. Clare, Ireland
Website: www.salmonpoetry.com
email: info@salmonpoetry.com

ISBN 1 903392 20 9

Cover photography by Ray Jeanotte
Cover design by Neil Farrell
Typeset by Siobhán Hutson
Printed by Offset Paperback Mfrs., PA

ABOUT THE AUTHOR

Ray Bradbury, American novelist, short story writer, essayist, playwright, screenwriter and poet, was born August 22, 1920 in Waukegan, Illinois. He graduated from Los Angeles High School in 1938. Although his formal education ended there, he became a 'student of life', selling newspapers on L.A. street corners from 1938 to 1942, spending his nights in the public library and his days at the typewriter to become a full-time writer in 1943, contributing numerous short stories to periodicals before publishing the collection, *Dark Carnival*, in 1947.

His reputation as a visionary writer was established with *The Martian Chronicles* in 1950, which describes the first attempts of Earth men to colonize Mars, and the unintended consequences. Next came *The Illustrated Man* and then, in 1953, *Fahrenheit 451*, which many consider to be Bradbury's masterpiece, a scathing indictment of censorship set in a future world where the written word is forbidden. In an attempt to salvage their history and culture, a group of rebels memorize entire works of literature and philosophy as their books are burned by the totalitarian state.

Other works include *The October Country*, *Dandelion Wine*, *A Medicine for Melancholy*, *Something Wicked This Way Comes*, *I Sing the Body Electric!*, *Quicker Than the Eye*, and *Driving Blind*. In all, Bradbury has published seventy-two books of short stories, poems, essays, and plays.

His new novel, *From the Dust Returned*, was published by William Morrow at Halloween 2001. Morrow will release *One More For the Road*, a new collection of Bradbury stories, in April, 2002.

Ray Bradbury's work has been included in three Best American Short Story collections. He has been awarded the O. Henry Memorial Award, the Benjamin Franklin Award, and the PEN Center USA West Lifetime Achievement Award.

In November 2000, the National Book Foundation Medal for Distinguished Contribution to American Letters was conferred upon Mr. Bradbury at the National Book Awards Ceremony in New York City.

Bradbury has been nominated for an Academy Award (for his animated film *Icarus Montgolfier Wright*), and has won an EMMY (for his teleplay of *The Halloween Tree*). He adapted sixty-five of his stories for television's Ray Bradbury Theater.

Married since 1947, Mr. Bradbury and his wife Maggie live in Los Angeles with four cats, four daughters and eight grandchildren.

ACKNOWLEDGMENTS

Acknowledgments are due to the publisher of the following collections where some of these poems were first published:

When Elephants Last in the Dooryard Bloomed. Knopf, 1973.

Where Robot Mice & Robot Men Run Round in Robot Towns. Knopf, 1977.

The Haunted Computer and The Android Pope. Knopf, 1981.

CONTENTS

TO IRELAND . . .

I dare not go – that isle has ghosts
And spectral rains along the coasts
Such rains as weep their loss in tears
Till I am drowned in sunken years.
When last I walked a Dublin street,
My gaze was clear, my pulses fleet,
Now half a life or more is gone
I cannot face sad Dublin's dawn.
The book clerks who once waited me
Are grey and gaunt, how can that be?
The hotel staff has up and fled,
Some stay as haunts, the rest are dead.
The candy butchers, beggars, maids,
Sleep out beyond in Maynooth's shades,
O'Connell's harpists? Gone to stay
Deep strewn along the hills of Bray.
Their happy faces smoke and stream
Across my life to shape each dream
So, Ireland? No, I'll not return
Where ghosts in smoking rainfalls burn.
Through Dublin I'll not stroll again
I cannot stand that haunted rain
Where youngness melts away to sea
And kills my soul, my heart, and me.

WHEN GOD IN LOINS A BEEHIVE PUTS

When boys are twelve or turned thirteen
A madness comes that's never been,
Then God in loins a beehive puts
A hive that rages, runs, and ruts;
And all about the countryside
Pale Jekyll boys grow hair like Hyde.
Strange gifts to girls they'd gladly bring
As roundabout they stab and sting,
And wound each other, fallen in clumps
Of wildly seized-on orchard-rumps,
Which under trees lie deep in grass,
There boys or girls all seem first class;
So roundabout the earth they sting
Anthills, ripe friends, oh, anything!
Gone blind with blushed hot blood and mad,
How can we list their lusts as bad?
Because their wee hives, thrived with bees
Do, honeycombing, seek and seize,
To day-by-day and hour-by-hour,
Re-pollinate this root, that flower
As, bursting full of rising saps,
They waken gummed-and-glued from naps,
To wonder at these churning yeasts
That year mere boastful boys to beasts,
Again, again! Until some morn when
The bad boys wake to find? They're – men!

IT'S NO-EXCUSES-NEEDED-
FOR-LIVING WEATHER

It's no-excuses-needed-for-living weather;
The sky is shaken clear,
The land is storm-cleansed bright,
The air is honed and keen,
The water cool,
And schools of thoughts swim by
Bright school on school.
No darkness in the shade,
No doubt in me;
Kiln-fired each desert flower,
Sun-fired each tree.
From out blue mouths of sky
Bright birds wheel, spin,
Their humming leans to joy,
From might-have-been.
So, wrapped in day's fine light,
I cry, "Enough!"
But know it is a lie.
More of this stuff:
White linen, woven sun,
Skies spelled with heather;
Thank Life, Thank God, Thank Christ,
It's no-excuses-needed-for-living weather!

MANET/RENOIR

How often Manet genuflects
To the soft sweet napes of women's necks,
While Renoir, painting, here directs
Our gaze to peach-fuzz frontal sex.
No matter. Rear view or facade?
For both I thank a loving God!

POEM FOR DAVID LEAN WAITING BEFORE DAWN, BEFORE SUNSET, FOR THE GOLDEN TIME OF LIGHT

To rise at three midnight is wise and best
To work and wait and waiting know no rest,
Until the furnace-fires which rise at morn
Show minted gold when all of time is born
And camera drinks it in, as flesh drinks light
And even warts and wrinkles color right.
In special time and hour when all that's seen
Forever after's called the Light of Lean.
For David more than most arose at three
To see much more than most directors see,
That instant when the sun thrusts up its brim
Apollo / Midas / Croesus was to him.
He camera-kept that birthing and that gold
To dye old actors flesh, no longer old.
At dawn 300 seconds. Sunset? less.
See Van Gogh light that floods to burn and bless
And tincture-taint and torch all grass to wheat
And change to coins each cobble in the street.
And newsboys in the dawn, bicycling by
Are gold of cheek and sungold proud of eye.
The moment's gone, the actors stripped of fire,
Do numbly act in drab and dour attire,
Their words dumb pebbles and not meteor shower
Until the sunset comes with burning hour,
Through waiting day and tea with actors wait
And David frets and fumes and checks the gate
Of camera to be sure that sunset light
Is loved and trapped before the dousing night.
300 seconds more! How bright the scene
And all of it a light that's named for Lean.

TO KNOW WHAT ISN'T KNOWN, THAT'S MINE

To know what isn't known, that's mine,
My job, refining blood
To find what's good and bad in it,
What in the quick cell lies,
What dies or lives or lingering
Provides the key where all the good stuff hides.
I do not know it, cannot find it, so I try
With words to jump the pheasants forth
And ere they fly
To reckon them with further words, describe their wings,
All simmers, sings.
What word for hummingbird,
What lie for dragonfly
For simple sea and sand and wind and sky
What Alexandrian couplet couples all, first try?
Or do I meadow-cast and stone, to clone myself as wheat
Or wandering overhill in mind, sink deep in clover-sea
That soundly sounding flounders soul and me?
My mind all ricochet where flinting words bombard
To flower the day and lard the night with sparks,
Yet merest breath is death if I but sneeze
And lose all dreams that nest in trees and bush
Unless I hush myself and tread the path.
All's dead or dying. One quick self-conscious bark,
Away all's flying. So softly does it,
Brer Fox says: listen, son, for it is so!
Sweet wanderer of words, lie low, lie low!

WHICH SHALL IT BE
A poem for H.G. Wells

Which shall it be? Cabell asked that
In THINGS TO COME.
Then H.G. WELLS gave quick response
To all that questioning.
Sink back in dust or, upstart, lust for Mars?
Lie back to rust or, restless, reach and, yes, now!
Touch the stars?
God's children's flesh which: win or lose?
Build fire-escapes in skies, climb stellar slopes
Or nose the earth and bury all our hopes.
Cabell says choose.
Dust, worms, forever's night for you, for me?
Or sweet eternal worlds beyond that sea
Of stars.
Speak, wanderers of dumb Earth.
Which shall it be?
Which shall it be?
Which shall it be!

I CARRY ALWAYS THE INVISIBLE

I carry always the invisible
The things I know but do not know
And try to find, with a blind hand
In that country of the blind
That is the mind and all its thought
And every inner change of weather.
I tether the changing of light
Every shifting of sunsets towards night,
All those half lighted dreams before dawn
I make poems, give them homes,
Of the heiroglyphed lawn where the dogs scribbled by
Writing futures in dawn-frosted clover,
Down it goes, or it dies.
Annie Over. Hear the cries. Annie Over,
A ball, all alone, climbs the sky,
Sent by loud boy unseen
To some girl on the green on the far side of noon.
I stash them away
To reread them some day in some winter where night
Comes at three, and my reason to be
Is a ball that's sky rover
Hurled invisibly high
From no hand to no catch,
It will stay there because
I can make the arc pause,
I cry freeze
And the ball in a poem
Stays suspended in trees
And will never come down.
So you see, it is true
I carry always the invisible to me
As you carry that invisible made visible in you.

RING THE BELLS BACKWARD: GIVE UP THE GUN

*Remembering the Japanese Samurai who in the 16th Century
threw away gunpowder and went back to the sword for 300 years!*

No more the gun,
No more the firing at dawn
The rattling of muskets round the town,
All now are given up and tossed
In rivers where the dream-machines
Are drowned and swiftly lost.
On bridges ceremoniously
Or brinks of running streams,
The powderhorns are plunged
And go to sea, and, with them all the dreams
Of men whose hands would shape that steel
Back into swords
And future wars conceal.
Let there be swords
Samurai lords say this, and it is so.
Back in the flames the loud-mouthed steel
Now goes to suffer change
And come again as blade
And all the ghosts of future conflicts laid
And put away three hundred years or more.
War, step on back! Obedient, war
Does so. And spear again goes out
Where gun did go.
Could they do this, and we not learn their rule?
Samurai's school gives answer to the fool.
We, longing, look at it, time-travel back,
And wish ourselves that lack that was their lack.
We would our weapons take and lose in deeps,
Where sleep the guns of men who bade
The weapons, sleep.

Can we do this with jets and bombs and fire.
But no, and no again, it can't be so.
Yet, agonized, midnight our souls
Admire
How marching feudal lords,
Gave up the gun, and musket fire
Took ten steps back,
And used their swords.

DUBLIN SUNDAY

It's a dim Dublin Sunday, and all stiff at Tea
In Hibernian silence, sits good wife and me
The plays and the movies? God! sold weeks ahead,
The Buttery Pub? Locked! Its bright spigots dead!
While around the Hotel, what was mist smokes to fog.
In the grate, one wee spark of a smothered turf log.
While the tea in the Arctic-white cups ebbs and slides
With a sound of cold surf down our Sunday insides.
And the mist and the fog burn to welters of rains,
That rinse the dark soots down the iced funeral panes.
And the last of the tarts lies adead on its plate
And the last of th turf snuffs and sinks in the grate,
And the last of the tea launders porcelain teeth
While down seethes the rain while the frost underneath
Whispers sermons on paleness and whiteness all day,
As the fog, mist, and rain age and leaden to gray.
And the statue folks dust in their winter dark clothes
While the rain, fog, and mist threaten afternoon snows.
In the midst of this muteness, the door squeals a creak,
And an old man steps in with a grin winter-bleak,
As he sucks a deep breath, stares at all, and speaks. Now:
"Are you getting," he smiles, "through this Sunday,
    somehow?"

BETTER THE BOY OF BEAUTY,
THAN UNWASHED UGLY ME

Death looked at me.
"Too plain, too simple,
Too bumped and ugly,
Much too leaning toward grotesque," he said.
My face burned red.
"But this one now..."
Death turned.
"O, see the fires of Youth, all beauty-burned
And flaming in his cheeks, fire-rose!
Do you suppose, eh, well, do you suppose
That if I asked the lad
He'd lie with me?"
"Oh, be my guest," I said.
"I'd rather he were blessed."
"With death?" Death said.
"Yes, death," I said. "Him dead.
Oh, better him than me.
I'm much too parboiled, pimpled, baked,
And scar-cake ruined, see?"
"Too true," said Death, "Ah, true, much thanks,
And surely true. I'm glad
So, Phillip," then he whispered,
"Oh come hither, darling lad,
Would you love lawns, long hours
With shovelings and pits and flowers . . .
This, your endeavor . . .
To bed marrowing the earth
Forever?"
Philip turned coy, and clever,
Said: "Maybe. I guess. Er, why not . . .
Yes!"
Death popped the Bright Fruit's soul

Swallowed the dear boy whole.
"Why, thank you, lad!" he cried.
Philip, devoured, died.

The breakfast was some forty years ago.
Remembering, I know,
The facts sum simply:
Philip was milk cream smooth.
I – pimply.
I wake, laughing still.
How come? Well, see?
Better the Boy of Beauty
Than
unwashed
ugly
. . . me.

TO ALL YOUR INNER SELVES BE TRUE

Never doubt, always *do*.
It will come to you then,
Without beckoning,
In reckoning with Hate,
Use joy or fun;
Any combination thereof.
In sum: Love.
No use hating if you don't love to hate,
It must be happily delicious.
The fun in Alice
Is malice.
Darkness is nutritious.
Give it a chew,
It surfaces all the meaning of Mean
In me and you.
Transversely: joy
Springs all the roots in the running boy,
Reverses trends in the suicide,
Breakfasts Jekyll, buries Hyde.
Its best of course: do combinations,
Creations set right in-between;
What's seen or guessed or just half-seen.
Blow out the light, then strike a match,
Lift hatch on old Pandora's trunk,
Let out midnight, then get drunk
On noontime ciders, mornings clover,
Be the rover of both hours,
The day that soars,
The dark that sours.
But this above all, listen, you,
To all your inner selves be true.
If midnight speaks, give it your ear,
Then hear the song that in the breeze

Stands all the Muses in the trees
Again: enjoy it all. Malicious?
Yes! and then let Good enact your wishes.
So roundabout with Yang and Yin
Devour your tail and know your sin.
Run swiftly then through all that's Not.
Scribble it down! or it's *forgot!*

B.B. REMEMBERED

Sunset comes sooner
Sunrise comes later,
The inner equator shifts,
The mind drifts from its central core,
The morning floor is colder,
The dreams older and older,
And suddenly you sleep till noon
And bed you down with the twilight moon,
The days are dwarves where once they towered
The nights have grown to a giant size,
The cries of the birds. Why must the loons
Pipe tunes that are funeral tunes
Why does the sun come up at one,
At three can that be the setting sun,
Why's it dwindling down to a single hour
When an old man's loving eye can flower,
Well, get me up and prop my head
And see that my eager eye is fed,
Teach while yet there's me to teach,
This Manet strand, that Monet beach
One hour? Enough. It just must do.
So tuck me in bed at half past two.
Tomorrow's dawn, one thirty-five?!
Sweet Jesus, look. I'm still alive.
Here comes the dusk at two eleven
Blink! There's Botticelli's heaven.
Today now, what. One forty-eight!
It's late, ungum my eyes, it's late.
The sun dies out at two o three
Light Van Gogh's sun to kindle me!
What, this at last? sun here, sun gone
Flint me my pictures, make a dawn!
Sun up, sun down in a single breath

But I drink fire in the mouth of death,
Michelangelo's, Turner's, El Greco's skies.
Finished. Stop my cries.
Last glorious sunburst! God! . . . shut my eyes.

REVIVERE, REX!

Scientists predict, with new gene-chromosome research, we may be able to repopulate the world with extinct generations of animals.
News Item

With Recombinant DNA recall from dust
The beasts that once were ours to keep in trust;
Shape Mammoth fresh and new as on that morn
When all the flesh of ancient Time was born.
Rebuild the pterodactyl, give him flight,
Erect Tyrannosaurus at midnight,
Wake brontosaurus drowned in tarpit deeps,
Go tiptoes where the eohippus sleeps.
Then with your recombinant DNA's
Thrive slimes and muds where stegosaurus stays.
Be God, provoke His Medicines, cry, "Light!"
And all the lost beasts, waked, raise up from night.

Ecologists, beware! Observe our theses!
You Doomsters now our prime endangered Species!

I HAVE ENDURED MUCH TO REACH THIS PLACE

I have endured much to reach this place in time
Yet I have not been sick, nor mad,
Nor ruined in a wreck.
And yet I feel I have.
There is a thing in me, the walls of cells are thin,
My veins are glass, my heart the merest whim
Of beat and pause and beat,
Deaths in the street are mine. I would not have it so.
I know much more than I would want to know.
The breakfast headlines tell me of a war,
I know they die out there; put down my spoon.
Men land on the moon tonight, I know their joy,
The boy in me goes with them as they tread
Far overhead on dust world beyond reach
They teach my tired blood to love again.
There's rain in downtown Peru tonight,
I wash my face in it. In Indo China, one more massacre,
I run a race in it and lose.
You see?
I cannot *choose* to be or not to be.
Light, dark, high. low, or in between,
I've been the way the world was just this morn,
When things are born I am reborn,
When all things given are taken away,
I end my day forlorn, with no control,
My only role is getting it all down,
Before the damned stuff drowns me
In delight
Or stuffs me in a box for that long night
Which has no end.
Long lived, short fused,
I feel I'm used by Gods abandoned here
To act a fear and then enact reliefs

Their beliefs mine, but what are their beliefs?
To change their bloody togas once a moon
And dance without their clothes on Green Town's noon.
Their flesh invisible, and yet I see,
Their tragedies and triumphs
Where I stand free and open to their days,
To be a sluice or chimney for their ways.
Born to be knocked and broken, then to mend,
Or why else send me?
Commend the gods for making me so frail.
Then sit you down with wine:
I'll tell a tale.
What does the flea's fart feign to show and mean?
When beggars die, there are no Comets seen.

AHAB AT THE HELM

It looked extremely rocky for the Melville nine that day,
The score stood at two lowerings, with one lowering
    yet to play,
And when Fedallah died and rose, and others did the same
A pallor wreathed the features of the patrons of this Game.

A straggling few downed-oars to go, leaving behind the rest,
With that hope which springs eternal from the blind
    dark human breast.
They prayed that Captain Ahab's rage would thrust,
    strike, overwhelm!
They'd wager "Death to Moby!" with old Ahab at the helm.

But Flask preceded Ahab, and likewise so did Stubb,
And the Flask former was a midget, while the latter was
    a nub.
Behold! the stricken multitudes in silence pent did swoon,
For when, oh when would Ahab rise to hurl his dread
    harpoon?!

First Flask let drive a gaffing hook. The wonderment of all!
Then much-despised Stubb's right arm brought blood
    and bile and gall!
But when the mist had lifted, Ishmael saw what had
    occurred:
Flask stood safe in the second boat, while Stubb clutched
    to the third.

Then from the gladdened whaling-men went up a
    joyous yell,
It bounded from the tidal hills and echoed in the dell,
It struck upon the soaring wave, shook Pequod's mast
    and keel,
For Ahab, mighty Ahab, was advancing with his steel.

There was ease in Ahab's manner as he stepped into
    his place,
There was pride in Ahab's bearing and a smile on Ahab's face;
The cheers, the wildest shoutings, did not him overwhelm,
No man in all that crowd could doubt, 'twas Ahab at
    the helm.

Four dozen eyes fixed on him as he coiled the hempen rope,
Two dozen tongues applauded as he raised his steel,
    their hope.
And while the writhing Moby ground the whale-boats
    with his hip,
Defiance gleamed from Ahab's eye, a sneer curled Ahab's lip.

And now the white-fleshed monster came a-hurtling
    through the air,
While Ahab stood despising it in haughty grandeur there!
Close by the sturdy harpooner the Whale unheeded sped –
"That ain't my style," said Ahab. "Strike! Strike!"
    Good Starbuck said.

From the longboats black with sailors there uprose a
    sullen roar,
Like the beating of mad storm waves on a stern and
    distant shore:
"Kill Starbuck! Kill the First Mate!" shouted someone
    at the band.
And its likely they'd have done so had not Ahab raised
    his hand.

With a smile of Christian charity great Ahab's visage shone,
He stilled the rising tumult and he bade the Chase go on.
He signalled to the White Whale, and again old Moby flew.
But still Ahab ignored it. Ishmael cried, "Strike! Strike,
    man!" too.

"Fraud!" yelled the rebel sailors, the sea-echoes answered,
   "Fraud!"
But one scornful glance from Ahab and his audience
   was awed.
They saw his face grow pale and cold, they saw his
   muscles strain,
And they knew that Ahab's fury would not pass that
   Whale again.

The sneer is gone from Ahab's lips, his teeth are clenched
   in hate,
He pounds with cruel violence his harpoon upon his pate,
And now old Moby gathers power, and now he lets it go.
And now the air is shattered by the force of Ahab's blow!

Oh, somewhere on the Seven Seas, the sun is shining bright,
The hornpipe plays yet somewhere and somewhere
   hearts are light;
And somewhere teachers laugh and sing, and somewhere
   scholars shout,
But there is no joy in Melville – mighty Ahab has
   Struck Out.

WITH LOVE
For Leonard Bradbury

My father ties, I do not tie, my tie.
On some night long ago, in June
I tried to try
My first tie snarled upon my vest,
My hands all thumbs,
And presto-chango,
Something Awful This Way Comes.
My father quietly came by
And studied me and stood behind.
"Be blind," he said.
"Stay off of mirrors.
Let your fingers
Learn to do."
His lesson lingers. What he said was true.
Eyes shut,
With him to help me over-up, around and under-out
Somehow a knot miraculous came about.
"There's nothing to it," said my Dad.
"Now, son, you do it. No; eyes shut."
And with one last dear blind perceiving
He taught my crippled fingers
Arts of weaving. Then, turned away.
Well, to this day, how dare I boast,
I cannot do it.
I call that long-gone sweet-tobacco-smelling ghost
To help me through it.
He helps me yet;
Upon my neck, his breath, the scent of his last cigarette.
There is no death, for yestereve
His phantom fingers came and helped me tuck and weave.
If this is true (it is!) he'll never die.
My father ties, I do not tie, my tie.

ALL FLESH IS ONE; WHAT MATTERS SCORES?

The thing is this:
We love to see them on the green and growing field;
There passions yield to weather and a special time;
There all suspends itself in air,
The missile on its way forever to a goal.
There boys somehow grown up to men are boys again;
We wrestle in their tumble and their ecstasy,
And there we dare to touch and somehow hold,
Congratulate, or say: Ah, well, next time. Get on!
Our voices lift; the birds all terrified
At sudden pulse of sound, this great and unseen fount,
Scare like tossed leaves, fly in strewn papers
Up the wind to flagpole tops:
We Celebrate Ourselves!
We play at life, we dog the vital tracks
Of those who run before and we, all laughing, make
    the trek
Across the field, along the lines,
Falling to fuse, rising amused by now-fair, now-foul
Temper-tantrums, spring-leaps, handsprings, recoils,
And brief respites when bodies pile ten high.
All flesh is one, what matter scores;
Or color of the suit
Of if the helmet glints with blue or gold?
All is one bold achievement,
All is a fine spring-found-again-in-autumn day
When juices run in antelopes along our blood,
And green our flag, forever green,
Deep colored of the grass, this dye proclaims
Eternities of youngness to the skies
Whose tough winds play our hair and re-arrange our stars
So mysteries abound where most we seek for answers.
We do confound ourselves.

All this being so, we do make up a Game
And pitch a ball and run to grapple with our Fates
On common cattle-fields, cow-pasturnings,
Where goals are seen and destinies beheld,
And scores summed up so that we truly know a score!
All else is nil; the universal sums
Lie far beyond our reach,
In this wild romp we teach our lambs and colts
Ascensions, swift declines, revolts, wild victories,
Sad retreats, all compassed in the round
Of one October afternoon.
Then winds, incensed and sweet with dust of leaves
Which, mummified, attest the passing of the weather,
Hour, day, and Old Year's tide,
Are fastened, gripped and held all still
For just one moment with the caught ball in our hands.
We stand so, frozen on the sill of life
And, young or old, ignore the coming on of night.

All, all, is flight!
All loss and ept recovery.
We search the flawless air
And make discovery of projectile tossed
The center of our being.
This is the only way of seeing;
To run half-blind, half in the sad, mad world,
Half out of mind –
The goal-line beckons,
And with each yard we pass,
We reckon that we win, by God, we win!
Surely to run, to run and measure this,
This gain of tender grass
Is not a sin to be denied?
All life we've tried and often found contempt for us!
So on we hied to lesser gods
Who treat us less as clods and more like men

Who would be kings a little while.
Thus we made up this mile to run
Beneath a late-on-in-the-afternoon-time sun.
We chalked aside the world's derisions
With our gamebook's rulings and decisions.
So divisions of our own good manufacture
Staked the green a hundred yards, no more, no less.
The Universe said "No"?
We answered, running, "Yes!"

Yes to Ourselves!
Since naught did cipher us
With scoreboards empty,
Strewn with goose-egg zeros
Self-made heroes, then we kicked that minus,
Wrote in plus!
The gods, magnanimous,
Allowed our score
And noted, passing,
What was less is now, incredibly, more!
Man, then, is the thing
Which teaches zeros how to cling together and add up!
The cup stood empty?
Well, now, look!
A brimming cup.

No scores are known?
Then look down-field,
There in the twilight sky the numbers run and blink
And total up the years;
Our sons this day are grown.

Why worry if the board is cleared an hour from now
And empty lies the stadium wherein died roars
Instead of men,
And goalposts fell in lieu of battlements?
See where the battle turf is splayed
Where panicked herds of warriors sped by,
Half buffalo and half ballet.
Their hoofmarks fill with rain
As thunders close and shut the end of day.
The papers blow.
Old men, half-young again, across the pavements go
To cars that in imagination
Might this hour leave for Mars.
But, sons beside them silent, put in gear,
and drive off towards the close of one more year,
Both thinking this:
The game is done.
The game begins.
The game is lost.
But here come other wins.
The band tromps out to clear the field with brass,
The great heart of the drum systolic beats
In promise of yet greater feats and trumps;
Still promising, the band departs
To leave the final beating of this time
To older hearts who in the stands cold rinsed with
autumn day
Wish, want, desire for their sons
From here on down, eternal replay on replay.

This thought, them thinking it,
Man and boy, old Dad, raw Son
For one rare moment caused by cornering too fast,
Their shoulders lean and touch.
A red light stops them. Quiet and serene they sit.
But now the moment is past.

Gone is the day.
And so the old man says at last:
"The light is green, boy. Go. The light is green."
They ran together all the afternoon;
Now, with no more words, they drive away.

THE MACHINES, BEYOND SHYLOCK

The Machines, beyond Shylock,
When cut bleed not,
When hit bruise not,
When scared shy not,
Lose nothing and so nothing gain;
They are but a dumb show:
Put Idiot in
And the moron light you'll know.
Stuff right, get right,
Stuff rot, get rot,
For no more power lies here
Than man himself has got.
Man his energy conserves?
Machineries wait.
Man misses the early train?
Then Thought itself is late.
Sum totalings of men lie here
And not the sum of all machines,
This is man's weather, his winter,
His wedding forth of time and place and will,
His downfall snow,
The tidings of his soul.
This paper avalanche sounds off his slope
And drowns the precipice of Time with white.
This tossed confetti celebrates his nightmare
Or his joy.
The night beginns an goes and ends with him.

EVIDENCE

Basking in sun,
Age 37, mid-Atlantic, on a ship,
And the ship sailing west,
Quite suddenly I saw it there
Upon my chest, the single one,
The lonely hair.
The ship was sailing into night.
The hair was white . . .
The sun had set beyond the sky;
The ship was sailing west,
And suddenly, O God, why, yes,
I felt, I knew . . .
So was I.

TELLING WHERE THE SWEET GUMS ARE

Even before you opened your eyes
You knew it would be one of those days.
Tell the sky what color it must be,
And it was indeed.
Tell the sun how to crochet its way,
Pick and choose among leaves
To lay out carpetings of bright and dark
On the fresh lawn,
And pick and choose it did.

The bees have been up earliest of all;
They have already come and gone
      and come and gone again
to the meadow fields
        and returned
      all golden fuzz upon the air
all pollen-decorated, epaulettes at the full,
       nectar-dripping.
Don't you hear them pass?
       hover?
       dance their language?
   Telling where the sweet gums are,
The syrups that make bears frolic and lumber in bulked
ecstasies,
That make boys squirm with unpronounced juices,
That make girls leap out of beds to catch from the
   corners of their eyes
Their dolphin selves naked
      aflash
      on the warm air
Poised forever in one
Eternal
Glass
Wave.

ONCE THE YEARS WERE NUMEROUS
AND THE FUNERALS FEW

Once the years were numerous and the funerals few,
Once the hours were years, now years are hours,
Suddenly the days fill up with flowers –
The garden ground is filled with freshdug slots
Where we put by our dearest special pets
And friends: wind-lost forget-me-nots.
Suddenly the obituary notices brim over,
The clover-wine they advertise is bitter in the bin:
Our friends put by from a great year when
The largest sin was the merest vice.
Old rice from weddings litters the autumn lawn;
No sooner arrived than gone on an Easter egg hunt
With an echo of daughters in flight. Their joyful hysteria!
In the night a clump of wisteria falls to the lawn in a wreath.
Our old cats underneath in the loam
Cry to come into our home. We won't let them.
We let the wind pet them and put them to sleep.
I look out at the street in the deep beyond three
And see going by on a bike the young beast
Who once dreamed he was me and then set out to be.
It's a nightful of ghosts, but then all nights are now.
It's a long way on until dawn.
I'm afraid to walk out on that lawn though it's flawless
        and green
With no holes and no flowers between,
And the morning birds drink the sweet dew
Where a treader might sink and be long lost to view
In those years that were numerous
And funerals few.

AIR TO LAVOISIER

Lavoisier, when just a boy,
Did suffer vital gas to joy;
He'd snuff a lung, he's sniff a quaff,
Then let it forth, much changed, to laugh
Which, echoed on the sides of seers
Who had not laughed in sixty years,
Convulsed their bones, ground them to dust
In hyperventilated lust.
And then, when grown, he sniffed the air,
That vital flux which everywhere
We lean upon with heart and lung,
And readied up a tune which, sung,
Changed Science's antique brass band.
Here's Oxygen, he said,
And on the other hand, here's Hydrogen;
They dance like gypsies down the strand
And in our blood these twin stuffs caper,
Half drunken gas, half flaming vapor.
So said Lavoisier's report;
Then stopped, he took another snort,
Cried, "Gods, one cannot get enough
Of this invigorating stuff!"
This secret to our Race bequeathing,
All cheered. Forgot.

But went on breathing.

WOMEN KNOW THEMSELVES; ALL MEN WONDER

Women know themselves;
All men wonder.
Women lie still with themselves;
Men and dogs wander.
Women appraise themselves;
Men must find.
Women have seeing eyes;
Men are blind.
Women stay, woman are;
Men would be, all men go yonder.
Women walk quietly;
Most men blunder.
Women watch cool mirrors
And there find mortal dust;
Men crave fast creeks
That break the sun and light
And shimmer laughter and show no sight
Save residues of lust;
So it is women accept
While men reject
The night.

Women bed down with child against the cold;
Men drink to shake the winter lodged in summer bones
Grow bold with beer
And thus more certainly
Grow old.

When death sighs whitening the sill
Women give way, cry welcome, stand still;
But men run fast
Thus racing for the hill
Where all lie lonely under stones
Where harvesters lie harvested by grass.

In sum: it is man's dear blind and blundered need
And begging after life
To break, to run, to leave;
And woman's to walk all warm with seed
All lit by candle-children
To look in midnight mirrors, finding truth,
And, happy in late years, recall,
And sometimes, grieve.

DARWIN, THE CURIOUS

Old Curious Charlie
He stood for hours
Benumbed,
Astonished.
Amidst the flowers;
Waiting for silence,
Waiting for motions
In seas of rye
Or oceans of weeds –
The stuff on which true astonishment feeds –
And the weeds that fed and filled his silo
With a country spread
By the pound or kilo,
Of miracles vast or microscopikc,
For them, by night, was he the topic?
In conversations of rye and barley,
Did they stand astonished
By Curious Charlie?

DARWIN, IN THE FIELDS

Darwin, in the fields, stood still as time
And waited for the world to now exhale and now
Take in a breath of wind from off the yield and swell
Of sea where fill the clouds with sighs;
His eyes knew what they saw but took their time to tell
This truth to him; he waited on their favor.
His nose kept worlds far larger than a goodly nose
    might savor
And waited for the proper place to fit the flavor in.
So eye and nose and ear and hand told mouth
What it must say;
And after a while and many and many a day
His mouth,
So full of Nature's gifts, it trembled to express,
Began to move.
No more a statue in the field,
A honeybee come home to fill the comb,
Here Darwin hies.
Though to ordinary eyes it might appear he plods,
Victorian statue in a misty lane;
All that is lies. Listen to the gods:
"The man flies, I tell you. The man flies!"

THE BOYS ACROSS THE STREET ARE DRIVING
MY YOUNG DAUGHTER MAD

The boys across the street are driving my young
    daughter mad.
The boys are only seventeen,
My daughter one year less,
And all that these boys do is jump up in the sky
and
beautifully
finesse
a basketball into a hoop;
But take forever coming down,
Their long legs brown and cleaving on the air
As if it were a rare warm summer water.
The boys across the street are maddening my daughter.
And all they do is ride by on their shining bikes,
Ashout with insults, trading lumps,
Oblivious of the way they tread their pedals
Churning Time with long tan legs
And easing upthrust seat with downthrust orchard rumps;
Their faces neither glad nor sad, but calm;
The boys across the street toss back their hair and
Heedless
Drive my daughter mad.
They jog around the block and loosen up their knees.
They wrestle like a summer breeze upon the lawn.
Oh, how I wish they would not wrestle sweating on
    the green
All groans,
Until my daughter moans and goes to stand beneath
    her shower,
So her own cries are all she hears,
And feels but her own tears mixed with the water.
Thus it has been all summer with these boys and my
    mad daughter.

Great God, what must I do?
Steal their fine bikes, deflate their basketballs?
Their tennis shoes, their skin-tight swimming togs,
Their svelte gymnasium suits sink deep in bogs?
Then, wall up all our windows?
To what use?
The boys would still laugh wild awrestle
On that lawn.
Our shower would run all night into the dawn.
How can I raise my daughter as a Saint,
When some small part of me grows faint
Remembering a girl long years ago who by the hour
Jumped rope
Jumped rope
Jumped rope
And sent me weeping to the shower.

IF ONLY WE HAD TALLER BEEN

The fence we walked between the years
Did balance us serene;
It was a place half in the sky where
In the green of leaf and promising of peach
We'd reach our hands to touch and almost touch that lie,
That blue that was not really blue.
If we could reach and touch, we said,
'Twould teach us, somehow, never to be dead.

We ached, we almost touched that stuff;
Our reach was never quite enough.
So, Thomas, we are doomed to die.
O, Tom, as I have often said,
How sad we're both so short in bed.
If only we had taller been,
And touched God's cuff, His hem,
We would not have to sleep away and go with them
Who've gone before,
A billion give or take a million boys or more
Who, short as we, stood tall as they could stand
And hoped by stretching thus to keep their land,
Their home, their hearth, their flesh and soul.
But they, like us, were standing in a hole.

O, Thomas, will a Race one day stand really tall
Aross the Void, across the Universe and all?
And, measured out with rocket fire,
At last put Adam's finger forth
As on the Sistine Ceiling,
And God's great hand come down the other way
To measure Man and find him Good,
And Gift him with Forever's Day?
I work for that.

Short man, Large dream. I send my rockets forth
    between my ears,
Hoping an inch of Will is worth a pound of years.
Aching to hear a voice cry back along the universal Mall:
We've reached Alpha Centauri!
We're tall, O God, we're tall!

THERE ARE NO GHOSTS IN CATHOLIC SPAIN

There are no ghosts in Catholic Spain.
What, none?
None! Nil!
It runs uphill against the grain of their religion.
In any region you might go
The rain in Spain falls on a ghostless plain.
On jaunts about Castille you'll find it so:
No haunts!
Those castles, ruined, empty-jawed, where gaunts
In England's guilt-prone nights might sprout,
In Spain are only filled with cat-footfalls of rain.
No ghosts are manufactured to weep here
Through doleful month or suffering year.
The dead, the good/bad church's dead?
(Learn it well.)
Jump straight to heaven! Bang!
Or:
Go to hell!

No Loitering, says Mother Church.
No reconnoitering on Earth's front porch.
Up you go: Angel's wings!
Down you go: Torch!
No ectoplasm whispering cold mirrors: "Alas!"
Pausing to admire
Its skull-face in the glass.
Up you jump: Cherub's breath!
Down you fall: Fire!
Not here: O, Lazarus, quit tomb, come forth!
He's long since blown north
On pagan winds toward colder climes.
Westminster's chimes do beckon him
To reckon with pale Protestants who boast

43

No English moat lacks skeletons,
Each tower? gives midnight snacks to ghost.
Gah, let the fools maunder!
Let their cold bods wander,
Lost in their own sleep,
Raking the rats awake and awash in the wainscot,
Making the old moldy flesh of lost London cold-creep,
Doubtful of heaven, uncertain of flames.
Let Hamlet's sire dropkick lost Yorick's skull downstairs
In winless games
For what gain?
Better the Catholic hush of soundless rain
Which falls in Spain upon a ghostless plain,
Where only the wind walks battlements
To touch and toll God's bell.
Again:
Good souls? To heaven!
Bad?
Go to hell.

THE BREAD OF BEGGARS, THE WINE OF CHRIST
Dublin, Christmas 1953

In Dublin's streets
Around the way to Christmas
Blackbirds sing.
Eire's orphan children cluster
Stashed in alleys, lost in sidewalks, cold in vestibules
    of movies
There to chant and carol through the snowing winds
In nights of rains.
Their high and weather-tossed refrains
Sound Christ and his sweet breath
His sun-birth, not his death:
His greeing forth of wisdom in the land
Sings forth down every street on every hand
Enchants your hotel room where echoes of it
Time your shaving before supper,
And as you leave the hotel door
More sparrows rise, more orioles
And blackbirds sing
From out the Christmas pies that celebrate a holy King.
The bread of beggars, the wine of Christ,
Delivered with the falling white, it manifests
A wonder, such miracles of snow that
Melting on small tongues
Become his sweetly breathing life.

You move to wife the weather
Husband winds that knife and harrow
Strike your marrow, freeze it pale.
Yet all about in storefront jails
Stunned flocks of starlings
Driven to earth in winter flood
Of fogging heaven, raining thunder, God who lids
    them down

And bids them sing for their lost souls.
And so they sing in promises of love not pain
A time that was, is not, but will arrive again
To warm the land and stir our bloods.
These hearths of children know all Dublin's neighborhoods
In every corner, alley, shop
Where snow drifts like spun-candles:
There they hide. Would you abide their place?
Then lift your touch to every heartbeat face
The bright coals of their cheeks breathe charcoal pink
As if the bellows of their tiny starling lungs
Blew on them forcing fire and ash
And fire once more.
From every winter door they cry a last refrain
To burn downwind;
With Christ a fever in their eyes
They birth him forth in snow that melts to rain
In Dublin's streets now once again
Hark! midnight church bells ring;
And echoing that sound of Christmas:
Blackbirds sing.

I LIVE BY THE INVISIBLE

Are we the Garden then?
And did we drive us forth to wilderness
Because we are both God and Given?
That is, the Beasts in which his breath enlivens
Self sustains
And shelters us from Death?
How can that be?
That Universe which constantly
Rehearses energies
And lets them shower in dazzling rains
Knows not itself, so must make things whose pains
And joys and jubilance
Incredibly persist. To say:
I see, I hear, I taste and tell! Exist!
A Blind Man taps the Eden walk
We are His cane
A Blind Man listens to the Void,
Our ears sustain Him in his aching vigilance.
A Blind Man reaches but finds Nil.
We reach for Him and flesh his Want and Will.
A Blind Man searches air to seek lost scents.
We breathe the sunrise wind and teach its relevance
To us and it and Him.
No matter Him or It or We?
We move persistently on Garden path
Away from dark and loss and rage and wrath
And if but one in three
Runs pell-mell on ahead
Who cares? Who'll say?
We play at taking turns, perhaps,
Now son, now daughter-bride,
Now Father-Mothering
The stuffs of Time

Which we devour.
Each second, minute, hour of quickened days
We banquet these to fire and fuel desire
To grow us tall in mirrow-maze.
Admire Ourselves in Him,
He in the threefold Us
From minussings of God – now Man the Plus.
I live by the invisible
The invisible is me.

REMEMBRANCE

And this is where we went, I thought,
Now here, now there, upon the grass
Some forty years ago.
I had returned and walked along the streets
And saw the house where I was born
And grown and had my endless days.
The days being short now, simply I had come
To gaze and look and stare upon
The thought of that once endless maze of afternoons.
But most of all I wished to find the places where I ran
As dogs do run before or after boys,
The paths put down by Indians or brothers wise and swift
Pretending at a tribe.
I came to the ravine.
I half slid down the path
A man with graying hair but seeming supple thoughts
And saw the place was empty.
Fools! I thought. O, boys of this new year,
Why don't you know the Abyss waits you here?
Ravines are special fine and lovely green
And secretive and wandering with apes and thugs
And bandit bees that steal from flowers to give to trees.
Caves echo here and creeks for wading after loot:
A water-strider, crayfish, precious stone
Or long-lost rubber boot –
It is a natural treasure-house, so why the silent place?
What's happened to our boys they now no longer race
And stand them still to contemplate Christ's handiwork:
His clear blood bled in syrups from the lovely
    wounded trees?
Why only bees and blackbird winds and bending grass?
No matter. Walk. Walk, look, and sweet recall.

I came upon an oak where once when I was twelve
I had climbed up and screamed for Skip to get me down.
It was a thousand miles to earth. I shut my eyes and yelled.
My brother, richly compelled to mirth, gave shouts
    of laughter
And scaled up to rescue me.
"What were you doing there?" he said.
I did not tell. Rather drop me dead.
But I was there to place a note within a squirrel nest
On which I'd written some old secret thing now
    long forgot.
Now in the green ravine of middle years I stood
Beneath that tree. Why, why, I thought, my God,
It's not so high. Why did I shriek?
It can't be more than fifteen feet above. I'll climb it handily.
And did.
And squatted like an aging ape alone and thanking God
That no one saw this ancient man at antics
Clutched grotesquely to the bole.
But then, ah God, what awe.
The squirrel's hole and long-lost nest were there.

I lay upon the limb a long while, thinking.
I drank in all the leaves and clouds and weathers
Going by as mindless
As the days.
What, what, what if? I thought. But no. Some forty
    years beyond!
The note I'd put? It's surely stolen off by now.
A boy or screech-owl's pilfered, read, and tattered it.
It's scattered to the lake like pollen, chestnut leaf
Or smoke of dandelion that breaks along the wind
    of time . . .
No. No.
I put my hand into the nest. I dug my fingers deep.
Nothing. And still more nothing. Yet digging further

I brought forth:
The note.
Like mothwings neatly powdered on themselves,
    and folded close
It had survived. No rains had touched, no sunlight bleached
Its stuff. It lay upon my palm. I knew its look:
Ruled paper from an old Sioux Indian Head scribble
    writing book.
What, what, oh, what had I put there in words
So many years ago?
I opened it. For now I had to know.
I opened it, and wept. I clung then to the tree
And let the tears flow out and down my chin.
Dear boy, strange child, who must have known the years
And reckoned time and smelled sweet death from flowers
In the far churchyard.
It was a message to the future, to myself.
Knowing one day I must arrive, come, seek, return.
From the young one to the old. From the me that was small
And fresh to the me that was large and no longer new.
What did it say that made me weep?

I remember you.
I remember you.

WHAT I DO IS ME – FOR THAT I CAME
for Gerard Manley Hopkins

What I do is me – for that I came.
What I do is me!
For that I came into the world!
So said Gerard;
So said that gentle Manley Hopkins.
In his poetry and prose he saw the Fates that chose
Him in genetics, then set him free to find his way
Among the sly electric printings in his blood.
"God thumbprints thee!" he said.
Within your hour of birth
He touches hand to brow, He whorls and softly stamps
The ridges and the symbols of His soul above your eyes!
But in that selfsame hour, full born and shouting
Shocked pronouncements of one's birth,
In mirrored gaze of midwife, mother, doctor
See that Thumbprint fade and fall away in flesh
So, lost, erased, you seek a lifetime's days for it
And dig deep to find the sweet instructions there
Put by when God first circuited and printed thee to life:
"Go hence! do this! do that! do yet another thing!
This self is yours! Be it!"
And what is that?! you cry at hearthing breast,
Is there no rest? No, only journeying to be yourself.
And even as the Birthmark vanishes, in seashell ear
Now fading to a sigh, His last words send you in the world:
"Not mother, father, grandfather are you.
Be not another. Be the self I signed you in your blood.
I swarm your flesh with you. Seek that.
And, finding, be what no one else can be.
I leave you gifts of Fate most secret; find no other's Fate,
For if you do, no grave is deep enough for your despair
No country far enough to hide your loss.

I circumnavigate each cell in you
Your merest molecule is right and true.
Look there for destinies indelible and fine
And rare.
Ten thousand futures share your blood each instant;
Each drop of blood a cloned electric twin of you.
In merest wound on hand read replicas of what I
    planned and knew
Before your birth, then hid it in your heart.
No part of you that does not snug and hold and hide
The self that you will be if faith abide.
What you do is thee. For that I gave you birth.
Be that. So be the only you that's truly you on Earth."

Dear Hopkins. Gentle Manley. Rare Gerard. Fine name.
What we do is us. Because of you. For that we came.

JOY IS THE GRACE WE SAY TO GOD

Joy is the grace we say to God
For His gifts given.
It is the leavening of time,
It splits our bones with lightning,
Fills our marrow
With a harrowing of light
And seeds our blood with sun,
And thus we
Put out the night
And then
Put out the night.
Tears make an end of things;
So weep, yes, weep.
But joy says, after that, not done . . .
No, not by any means. Not done!
Take breath and shout it out!
That laugh, that cry which says: Begin again,
So all's reborn, begun!
Now hear this, Eden's child,
Remember in thy green Earth heaven,
All beauty-shod:
Joy is the grace we say to God.

THEY HAVE NOT SEEN THE STARS

They have not seen the stars,
Not one, not one
Of all the creatures on this world
In all the ages since the sands first touched the wind
Not one, not one,
No beast of all the beasts has stood
On meadowland or plain or hill
And known the thrill of looking at those fires;
Our soul admires what they, oh, they, have never known.
Five billion years have flown in turnings of the spheres
But not once in all those years
Has lion, dog, or bird that sweeps the air
Looked there, oh, look. Looked there, ah God, the stars;
Oh, look, look there!
It is as if all time had never been,
Or universe or sun or moon or simple morning light.
Their tragedy was mute and blind, and so remains.
    Our sight?
Yes, ours? To know now what we are.
But think of it, then choose – now, which?
Born to raw Earth, inhabiting a scene
And all of it, no sooner viewed, erased, gone blind
As if these miracles had never been.
Vast circlings of sounding light, of fire and frost,
And all so quickly seen then quickly lost?
Or us, in fragile flesh, with God's new eyes
That lift and comprehend and search the skies?
We watch the seasons drifting in the lunar tide
And know the years, remembering what's died.

Oh, yes, perhaps some birds some nights
Have felt Orion rise and turned their flights
and turned southward
Because star-charts were printed in their sweet
    genetic dreams –
Or so it seems.
But see? But really see and know?
And, knowing, want to touch those fires
To grow until the mighty brow of man Lamarckiar-tall
Knocks earthquakes, striking moon,
Then Mars, then Saturn's rings;
And, growing, hope to show
All other beasts just how
To fly with dreams instead of ancient wings.
So, think on this: we're first! the only ones
Whom God has honored with his rise of suns.
For us as gifts Aldebaran, Centauri, homestead Mars.
Wake up, God says. Look there. Go fetch.
The stars. Oh, Lord, much thanks. The stars!

SCHLIEMANN

As Homer wrote, so Schliemann dreamed himself, half-blind,
To rise and go, to search, to find.
What centuries lost, young romance breached again,
And all against the intellect of men
Who said: mad boy, wild lad, give up your dreams
That dance by night
And shadow-show the eaves and ceiling light
With visions of high temples, shuffling cymbals,
Muffled drums;
But Schliemann turns in sleep, breaks forth a smile and
Lo! Troy comes!
Like head of David burst from marble brow,
Then neck, then monster shoulders like the prow
Of some carved boat that plows the wave!
So, beggar to all time, young Schliemann gave
More than we asked or wanted, knew or guessed;
And Troy in wave on wave and crest on crest
In stony tidal flow, like ancient sea
Now surfacing to sight surrounded he
Who dared to wonder, dream, and care to do
Unlike those men who soundless slept and no dream knew
He was the one to cry Troy's name by night
Then, searching lostness, find and set it right.

OF WHAT IS PAST, OR PASSING, OR TO COME

Of what is past, or passing, or to come,
These things I sense and sing, and try to sum.
The apeman with his cave in need of fire,
The tiger to be slain, his next desire.
The mammoth on the hoof a banquet seems,
How bring the mammoth down fills apeman's dreams.
How taunt the sabertooth and pull his bite?
How cadge the flame to end an endless night?
All this the apeman sketches on his cave
In cowards' arts that teach him to be brave.
So, beasts and fire that live beyond his lair
Are drawn in science fictions everywhere.
The walls are full of schemes that sum and teach,
To help the apeman reach beyond his reach.
While all his ape-companions laugh and shout:
"What are those stupid blueprints all about?
Give up your science fictions, clean the cave!"
But apeman knows his sketching chalk can save,
And knowing, learning, moves him to rehearse
True actions in the world to death reverse.
With axe he knocks the tiger's smile to dust,
Then runs to slay the mammoth with spear thrust;
The hairy mountain falls, the forests quake,
Then fire is swiped to cook a mammoth steak.
Three problems thus are solved by art on wall:
The tiger, mammoth, fire, the one, the all.
So these first science fictions circled thought
And then strode forth and all the real facts sought,
And then on wall new science fictions drew,
That run through history and end with . . . you.

THAT WOMAN ON THE LAWN

Sometimes, gone late at night,
I would awake and hear
My mother in another year and place
Out walking on the lawn so late
It must have been near dawn yet dark it was
The only light then in the gesture of the stars
Which wheeled around in motionings so soft
They took your breath to see; and there upon the grass
Like ghost with dew-washed feet she was
A maid again, alone, quite singular, so young.
I wept to see her there so strange,
So unrelate to me, so special to herself,
So untouched by the world, so evanescent, free,
With something wild come up in cheeks
And red to lips, and flashing in the eyes;
It frightened me.
Why should she wander out without permit,
Permission saying go or do not go
From us or any other . . . ?
Was she, or My God, wasn't she our mother?
How dare she walk, a virgin, fresh once more
Within a night that hid her face,
How dare displace us in her thoughts and will?!

And sometimes even still, late nights,
I think I hear her soft tread on the sill
And wake to see her cross the lawn
Gone wild with wishing, dreaming, wanting
And crouched down there until dawn,
Washing her hair with wind,
Paying no mind to the cold,
Waiting for some bold strange man
To rise up like the sun

And strike her beauteous-blind!
And weeping I call out to her;
Oh, young girl there,
Oh, sweet girl in the dawn!
I do not mind, no, no.
I do not mind.

GO NOT WITH RUINS IN YOUR MIND

Go not with ruins in your mind
Or beauty fails; Rome's sun is blind
And catacomb your cold hotel
Where should-be heaven's could-be hell.
Beware the temblors and the flood
That time hides fast in tourist's blood
And shambles forth from hidden home
At sight of lost-in-ruins Rome.
Think of your joyless blood, take care,
Rome's scattered bricks and bones lie there
In every chromosome and gene
Lie all that was, or might have been.
All architectural tombs and thrones
Are tossed to ruin in your bones.
Time earthquakes there all life that grows
And all your future darkness knows,
Take not these inner ruins to Rome,
A sad man wisely stays at home;
For if your melancholy goes
Where all is lost, then your loss grows
And all the dark that self employs
Will teem – so travel then with joys.
Or else in ruins consummate
A death that waited long and late,
And all the burning towns of blood
Will shake and fall from sane and good,
And you with ruined sight will see
A lost and ruined Rome. And thee?
Cracked statue mended by noon's light
Yet innerscaped with soul's midnight.
So go not traveling with mood
Or lack of sunligt in your blood,
Such traveling has double cost,

When you and empire both are lost.
When your mind storm-drains catacomb,
And all seems graveyard rock in Rome –
Tourist, go not.
Stay home.
Stay home!

BYZANTIUM I COME NOT FROM

Byzantium
I come not from
But from another time and place
Whose race is simple, tried and true;
As boy
I dropped me forth in Illinois,
A name with neither love nor grace
Was Waukegan. There I came from
And not, good friends, Byzantium.
And yet in looking back I see
From topmost part of farthest tree
A land as bright, beloved and blue
As any Yeats found to be true.
The house I lived in, hewn of gold
And on the highest market sold
Was dandelion-minted, made
By spendthrift bees in bee-loud glade.
And then of course our finest wine
Came forth from that same dandelion,
While dandelion was my hair
As bright as all the summer air;
I dipped in rainbarrels for my eyes
And cherries stained my lips, my cries,
My shouts of purest exaltation:
Byzantium? No. That Indian nation
Which made of Indian girls and boys
Spelled forth itself as Illinois.
Yet all the Indian bees did hum:
Byzantium.
Byzantium.

So we grew up with mythic dead
To spoon upon midwestern bread
And spread old gods' bright marmalade
To slake in peanut-butter shade.
Pretending there beneath our sky
That it was Aphrodite's thigh;
Pretending, too, that Zeus was ours
And Thor fell down in thundershowers.
While by the porch-rail calm and bold
His words pure wisdom, stare pure gold
My grandfather a myth indeed
Did all of Plato supersede;
While Grandmama in rocking-chair
Sewed up the raveled sleeve of care,
Crocheted cool snowflakes rare and bright
To winter us on summer night.
And uncles gathered with their smokes
Emitted wisdoms masked as jokes,
And aunts as wise as Delphic maids
Dispensed prophetic lemonades
To boys knelt there as acolytes
On Grecian porch on summer nights.
Then went to bed there to repent
The evils of the innocent
The gnat-sins sizzling in their ears
Said, through the nights and through the years
Not Illinois nor Waukegan
But blither sky and blither sun;
Though mediocre all our Fates
And Mayor not as bright as Yeats
Yet still we know ourselves. The sum?
Byzantium.
Byzantium.

WHY DIDN'T SOMEONE TELL ME
ABOUT CRYING IN THE SHOWER?

Why didn't someone tell me about crying in the shower?
What a fair fine place to cry,
What a rare place to let go
And know that no one hears –
Let fall your tears which, with the rain that falls,
Appall nobody save yourself, and standing there
You wear your sadness, properly assuaged,
Your head and face massaged by storms of spring
Or, if you think it, autumn rain.
You drain yourself away to naught, then move to joy;
But sadness must come first, it must be bought.
A thirst for melancholy, then, must find a place
To stand in corners and know grief;
The last leaf on the tree may turn you there,
Or just the way the wind, with cats,
Prowls down the garden grass,
Or some boy passing on a bike,
Selling the end of summer with a shout,
Or some toy left like doubt upon a walk,
Or some girl's smile that, heedless, cracks the heart,
Or that cold moment when each part and place and room
In all your house is empty, still,
Your children gone, their warm rooms chill,
Their summer-oven beds unyeasted, flat,
Waiting for cats to visit some half-remembered ghost
In the long fall.
So, for absolutely no good reason at all
Old oceans rise
One's eyes are filled with salt;
Something unknown then dies and must be mourned.
Then standing beneath the shower at noon or night
Is right and proper and good –

What was not understood now comes to hand . . .
One's interior land is wonderfully nourished by tears:
The years that you brought to harvest
Are properly scythed down and laid,
The games of love you played are ribboned and filed,
A whole life locked in your blood is thus let free, unbound.
So freely found then, know it, let it go
From out your eyes and with the sweet rains flow.

But now, good boys, strong gentlemen, take heed;
This stuff is not for women, lost, alone;
The need is yours as well as theirs.
Take women's wisdom for your own.
Take sorrow's loan and let your own cares free.
Christ, give it a try!
Not to learn how to weep is, lost fool,
But to learn how to die.
Stand weeping there from midnight until morn,
Then from impacted wisdom shorn, set free,
Leap forth to laugh in freshborn Children's Hour and shout:
Oh, damn you, maids, that's what it's all about?!
Sweet widows with your wisdom, blast you all to hell!
Why?
Why, why, God, oh why,
Why wouldn't someone tell me about crying in the shower?

THAT SON OF RICHARD III

Moby Dick was two books written between February 1850 and
August 1851. The first book did not contain Ahab. It may not,
except incidentally, have contained Moby Dick. Somewhere
along the way to writing a book about the Whale Fishery,
Melville found and bought a seven-volume set of Shakespeare's
plays. He reported on his find to his editor:

> *It is an edition in glorious great type, every letter whereof is a*
> *soldier, & the top of every 't' like a musket barrel. I am mad to*
> *think how minute a cause has prevented me hitherto from reading*
> *Shakespeare. But until now copy that was come-at-able to me*
> *happened to be a vile small print unendurable to my eyes which*
> *are tender as young sperms. But chancing to fall in with his*
> *glorious edition, I now exult over it, page by page.*

Whereupon, Melville tossed his first version of The Whale
overboard and vomited forth the novel that we now know as
Moby Dick.

At first there were but whales
And now a Whale.
At first there was but sea and tides by night
But now the fountains of Versailles somehow set sail
And sprinkled all the vasty deeps at three a.m.
With souls' pure jets.
At first there was no captain to the ship
Which, named Pequod,
Set sail for destinations, not for God.
But: God obtruded, rose and blew his breath
And Ahab rose, full born, to follow Death,
Know dark opinions,
Seek in the strangest salt dominions for one Beast
And from what was a simple-minded breakfast,
O Jesus mild and tempered sweetments,
Now a Feast!

How came it so?
That from such crumbs tossed forth at morning
Such nightmare terrors grow,
What was a cat-toy lost upon old summer lawns
Has through one season grown to monster size
To panic-color all gray Melville's dawns?

Why, Willie happened by!
That is the end, the explanation, and the all.
As blind almost as Homer, Herman never read
The good or bad or in-between Othello
The dead put down by Richard Third,
Iago's boast,
Never, gone out at midnight in his mind,
Had Ahab with a small a
Stumbled and fallen blind against
Mad Hamlet's father's murdered ghost.
But now, in seven volumes of large size
And large, O gods, the font of type,
The words, the trumpetings of metaphor and doom:
All that was microscopic filled his room,
All that had filled his room now filled his mind
From south to west then east and now the panicked North.
Shakespeare beneath his window gave his shout:
"O Lazarus! Herman Melville! Truly come ye forth!
And what's that with you?
Dreadful gossamer?
Funeral wake? or Arctic veil?"
"What, this? Why, Jesus lily-of-the-valley breath,
It seems to be . . .
A Whale!"

And what a whale! A true born Beast of God.
Shakespeare stood back away
As Herman trod a path and made a launching-spot, a maze
Wherein to lose then find titanic Moby

And then send him down the ways!
And then an ancient King came forth to stand with Will
And call along the tide of Time down hill upon the wind
And tear his beard and rend his sanity,
Disclaim his daughters, curse all midnight Fates.
So Lear and his progenitor gave cry
And from an Arctic miracle of waters
A white shape formed to panic and to most delicious
    fright,
A whale like all Antarctica, dread avalanche of dawn at night
Ribbed, skinned, then stuffed with lights and soul
    filched out of Lear
Sailed, submarine, through Richard Third's wild dreams,
Touched Verne, and maddened Freud and kept our schemes,
Those schemes American which were, while awed,
To question all the malt that Milton drank while
    sipping God.
God, Nature, Space, all Time, now stand aside, we said.
The Whale, in answer, gasping, fluming Universal breath
Rushed at us like a marbled tomb, his spout one bloody
    fount of Death.
And rammed and sank our hubris, fluked our pride.
The waters shut and closed on all who died that day
    on the Pequod.
So the American men, each one proclaimed self-king
Took their blasphemies beneath the monstrous watering
While Ahab wrapped in hemp upon his cumbrous bride
Still beckoning to us to follow, worry, harrow
Those tracks that watery vanish on the instant trod,
With one last outraged cry, a fisting wave,
Sank from our view with God.

So Melville in his inner deeps did dive
To find the shroud, the ghost, the thing alive
Iin all the flesh that, aged, shadowed, dead
Most wanted issue, to be found, known, read,

And on the lawns of Avon took his stance
To join the Bard in festive, antic dance.
And to the morning window of old Will
As morn came up and dusk went down the sill
Cried out, O Lazarus William Shakespeare,
Come you forth in whale!
And Will all fleshed in marble white
Could not prevail against such summonings and taunts,
And slid him forth in size for jaunts to break a continent,
Sink Armadas in the tides.
So Shakespeare glides forever in dread comet tails
That shine the Deeps,
He prowls that mutual subterrane
Where Melville/God's truth starts and wakes from
    murdered sleeps.

Thus from his antique caul, his bloody veil
Old Willie William, long gone dust in jail,
Was clamored forth to freedom in a Whale
That swam all thunders, rumors, plunders in the morn,
Insurance that good Shakespeare, now reborn,
Would live two lives, the one he'd had before
But now another chance to make less More.
From blubbers, metals, renderings he rose
To dress plain-suited Melville in fresh clothes,
Such clothes as foreskin whale-prick metaphors can
    make and sell,
Ilumine Heaven and relight the coals of Hell.
So Shakespeare, boned and fleshed and marrowed deep
Did waken Melville from whale-industries of sleep
To run on water, burn St. Elmo's fires,
And shape cathedral spires from Moby's tidal rib-cage
    tossed to shore
And again and again from less make feasts of More.
What was mere oil of spermaceti now became
Anointments for a Papal brow in Sweet Christ's name

Pronounced from drippings of fused universal mask
    and face,
What first was simple journeying became a Chase.
So off and round the world ran two men, wild,
Skinned in one Lazarus flesh, one loud, one mild,
Each summoning the other,
And neither knowing which was elder, therefore
    evil-wiser brother
Until – Flukes out! Black blood!
From mutual toil
They brought a miracle of fish to boil;
Like God who spoke and uttered Light,
These twins in unison said Night
And there was Night;
That night in which great panics birthed and hid,
That dawnless hour from which old Moby slid
And knocked the world half off its axis into awe
And all because Dear Willie stuck his metaphor down
    Herman's craw!

THE SYNCOPATED HUNCHBACKED MAN

The syncopated hunchbacked man
He moves in rhythms all his own,
The bone along his back does this to him,
He moves then to a private inner whim
A hymn to cartilage, a spine that broke
By sheer genetics in the womb, God's hidden joke;
So balled into the world he came and soon or late
His shellcrab shoulders taught his bones to syncopate
And pat and shuffle on the street as if to fling
Him in a rigadoon of spring; he comes
And pressured is his mouth in whines and hums;
A *Gloria* perhaps to chromosome
That built him from cracked bricks, a cramping home
In which his soul like doll is stuffed in house
The house a caving roof, his soul crazed mouse
That hides in blood then rushes and collides
With yet more crumpled bone, a rodent mad
With gyrating, while up above? A face that's glad.
A mask? But no. The hunchback loves the fall,
The summer, winter, spring, he takes it all,
It's one romance;
And where his spine taught him to shuffle-tap
    and syncopate
Now realer dance does seize his feet
And in the ecstasy of life, goes down the street.
So Being, if even it's hunched, finds recompense
And dearly loves June miracles immense;
For Christ himself, who knows?, once shared this lack:
Born, lived, laughed, wept, and died, with crumpled back.

IF MAN IS DEAD, THEN GOD IS SLAIN

What size is Space? A thimble!
No! Outside of a Sun!
The nimble tricks of lightning,
Dichotomies lost, won;
Black holes in which, sequestered,
Great nightmares stride the beams,
Sun-spots in which gods, festered,
Give up their fractured dreams.
What is this dream of Cosmos,
What's birthed from Panic's plan?
A mad brave wingless bird-thing,
This beast half-grown to Man.
Born from a senseless yearning
Of molecules for form,
Birthed from a mindless burning
Of solar fire-storm –
The Universe, in needing,
Made flesh of empty space,
And with a mighty seeding
Made pygmy human race . . .
Which now on fires striding
Walks up the stars to live
And cry to God in hiding:
We birth ourselves! Forgive!
Then from the Cosmos breathing,
An answering word from Him:
"No, dwarf-child, self-bequeathing,
I birthed you as a whim.
I laughed you from the darkness,
I dropped you as a joke,
But strange, small, fragile, creature,
You fell but never broke!
And now I see you laughing

As if the jokes were yours;
Perhaps we made each other
In some wild common cause
So let us share a hubris,
Take common flesh as bread,
And drink each other's laughter,
Fall from each other's bed.
But careful, darling monster,
Your laugh might crack your soul,
What's yours is mine, remember,
We separate, are Whole."
God laughs, and Man gives answer,
Man laughs and God responds;
Then off they glide on rafters
Of stars like skating-ponds.
And which is God, which Human,
God now must truly say:
We fly much like each other,
We walk a common clay.
I dreamed Man into being,
He dreams me now to stay –
Twin mirror selves of seeing,
We live Forever's Day.
If Man should die I'd blindly
Rebirth that Beast again;
I cannot live without him.
Man dead? Then God is slain!
My Universe needs seeing,
That's Man's eternal task,
What is the use of being,
If God is but a mask?"
So, Man and God, conjoining,
Are One, uncelibate,
And spawn the Cosmic rivers,
In billions celebrate
No Ending or Beginning,

No crease, stitch, fold or seam;
Where God leaves off, Man's starting
To recompense the Dream.
Behold! the Mystery stirring . . .
Here comes the human moles!
To rise behind God's masking
And peek out from the holes.

LONG THOUGHTS ON BEST-SELLERS
BY WORST PEOPLE

Oh, the bad that I've demolished, they are doing far too well,
And the bores that I have vanquished now have learned
    new ways to spell;
For the alphabet of tombstones, once it's learned, can set
    you free,
So these nonbook, awful writers now turn up to blab at tea.
Lo, the Fascists and the Commies, Nixon's Plumbers
    in a Clan,
All the jet-set hostage-killers that forever frighten man,
Clang their death-bells, shriek for banknotes, every night
    upon my lawn
After all my time invested to make super-sure they'd gone.
For from Hell where I had sent them now the driveling
    fiends return
In the vapored rains of fire where dire Savonarolas burn,
Here come Sirhan Sirhan cabals, Senate Girl-Friends
    whose élan
Marches Dante down the sludgeways where new novels
    hit the fan.
Here Mad Donkey, sad Behemoth (G.O.P. upon his flank)
Ballot-stuffers, candle-muffers of the meanest row and rank,
Here runs night-train bearing Lenin, there kind Stalin
    and his mob,
Here, reprinted, Adolf's Bunker: Mayor Daley (Lyndon's slob),
Hail, John Dean, John Mitchell, Agnew – live best-sellers
    in the stalls,
While more lecturing assassins fill our cities' concert halls.
So, in death there seems much living, and in evil mostly good.
Otherwise why do these demons Watergate my neighborhood?

And, more books about young Edward sunk near
    Chappaquiddick Bridge,
One more second-gunman theory on the Dallas
    Book-Tower ridge!
Linda Lovelace, be our teacher, Hustler Flynt now be
    our scribe,
Martin Bormann, Hess and Goebbels, all's forgiven!
    Lead our tribe!
Orwell taught us black was whiter if you stood upon
    your head,
Now we know that white is blacker and what's most
    alive is dead.
All kidnappers and skyjackers, get you home and
    write a book!
But be sure the title reads as: *Heck, You Know That
    I'm No Crook.*
Franco's dead – Ah, God, the wonder! Look! Loud
    Mussolini's gone!
But ten books about these monsters will be done and
    out by dawn!

I'll retire me to Bedlam, for my goodnes is my shame,
I'll hire some evil Berlitz, teach myself a smarter game,
Run with dogs and hogs and butchers, make Caligula
    my name;
Vote for Nixon, Mao, Castro, Idi Amin, James Early Ray.
Buy a bedsheet, cut some eyeholes, join the Book Club KKK.
Kill Olympic sports for breakfast, burn an airport,
    see the sights!
Then send cables, ask for bidders, sell the film and TV rights.
Princess Di is ripe for sequels, flood the market, what the hell.
Since the bad that I once vanquished, still around,
    are doing well.

COME WHISPER ME A PROMISE

1.

Come whisper me a promise,
Come sit upon my stone,
Come lean the winds of autumn
And say me not alone.
Come tell me of Tomorrow
When I will come reborn
Forgetful of All Hallows
And fresh with Christmas Morn.
Come say I'll live forever,
And skull and bones not mine,
Come prove that graves are shallow
Where God but saves old wine,
And bottles souls and bins them
In vintages gone fine.
Come say that tombs are balsa
As light as thistledown,
And all God needs is whistle
And we are swiftly flown –
A milkweed ectoplasm
That, tossed, fills Universe
At these Words from His mouthing:
"Stand tall! All Time, reverse!"
Take on new flesh and knowing,
Forget that lengthy Dust,
Rise up in mad bells pealing
In feverings, fresh lust,
To cover stars and shape them
Far livelier than fires,
To honeycomb and seed-wind,
To all that God admires.
Be Son, Be Daughter, flying,
Where Time stops, start it up!
At every star-hole, crying,

Thrust Life and fill the cup.
Cut this for me on gravestone?
Speak this into my grave?
Yes, future children, hear me:
Tell old man to be brave
While waiting years of fallow
Until with young man's cry
Say: Ghost, good Time's your saviour,
God will not pass you by.
He holds you in His reckon,
All's kept, re-used, all's thrift,
With new womb bright he'll beckon
From old tomb birth Life's gift.
From dust and death commingled
He take dark flints to smite
And from your bones, thus smitten –
Lo!
Ten billion years of Light!

THE OLD MAN WAKES

The old man wakes
Because the young boy capering his blood
Has jarred his wits, disloged old melancholies
Which now teem and brood and wash his life away.
Being old, he thinks, is not so bad
If being young would only go and leave one quite alone.
But still that wild lad jumps and snorts,
Cavorts the fences, climbs to fiercely hug the trees,
Digs tunnel earthworks, bloodies knees,
Shouts from housetops, pisses off of roofs,
Drums the lawns of morning with his stallion hooves,
Runs down the middle of all's lost, yet-to-be-found
Dawn's streets
To meet the storm-cloud, self-contained,
Which crowns in thunders and darkly arriving
Nightmare locomotive circus train
Bringing its sweet and sour, shadow and light.
So the boy's world, with its evil and good
Has been turning all night on its shoulder,
Restless in slumber. Now elephants lumber
With sun on their granite and boulder-hewn precipice hides,
And all immense Time in their timbers,
The sun rises. Dawn slides on a forest that walks
A shambling of boughs and grey limbs,
While in the red sky all gyres and hymns some last star
Now sings: Light!
In sinking remembrance, the old man then hears
    himself groan:
You, boy! or Christ help me! don't leave me alone!
I lied! I never once meant the dumb words that I said:
"I wish you were dead! I wish you were gone!
Get out of my blood! Go bother some other
New bright neighborhood!"
No, sweet lad, stay! For in your voice I hear

The green root tunnel to retrieve some year
I had long forgotten, may have never known
In a land snowed under, in a time now flown.
Leap back with a shout, boy, breathe me your weather.
Run, who once was me, O good green twin, forgive,
Live, your old self says: pole-vault my mind, swim in my blood.
So let us bed . . . together.